A REAL MEN

desıred

/dɪˈzʌɪəd/

adjective

adjective: **desired**

1. strongly wished for or intended.

"the bribe had its desired effect"

desire

/dɪˈzʌɪə/

verb

past tense: **desired**; past participle: **desired**

1. strongly wish for or want (something).

"he never achieved the status he so desired"

sinonimi:

wish for, want, long for, yearn for, crave, set one's heart on, hanker after/for, pine for/after, thirst for, itch

for, be desperate for, be bent on,
have a need for, covet, aspire to;

antonimi:
unwanted

• want (someone) sexually.
"there had been a time, years
ago, when he had desired her"

sinonimi:
be attracted to, lust after, burn for,
be captivated by, be infatuated by;

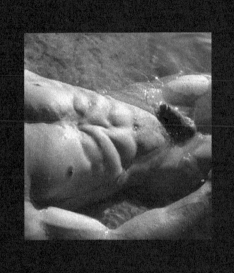

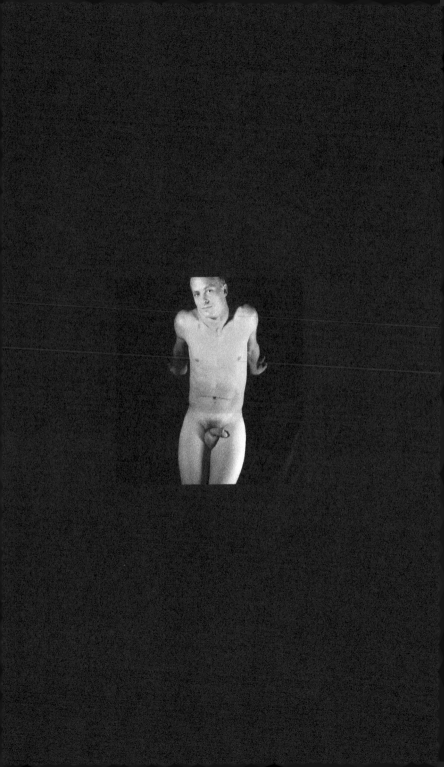

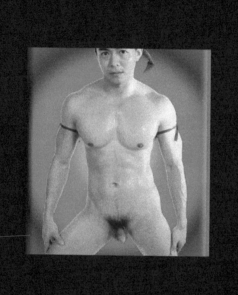

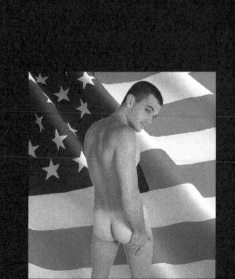

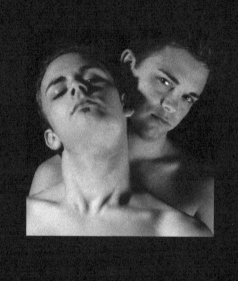

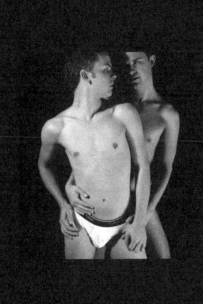

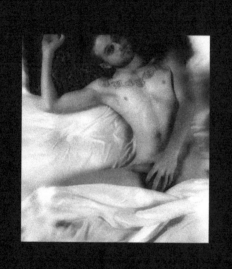

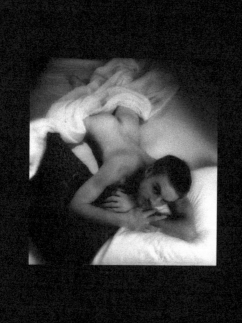

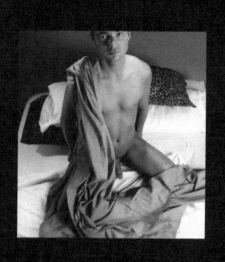

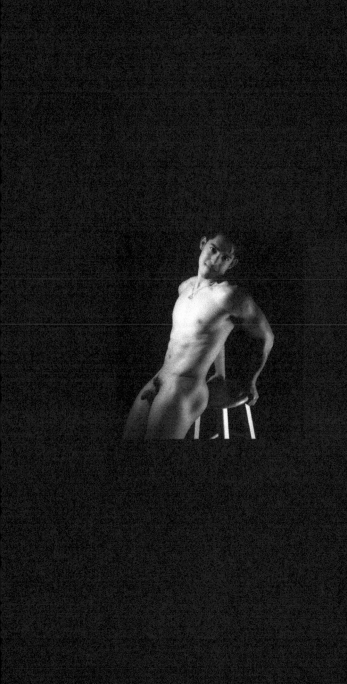

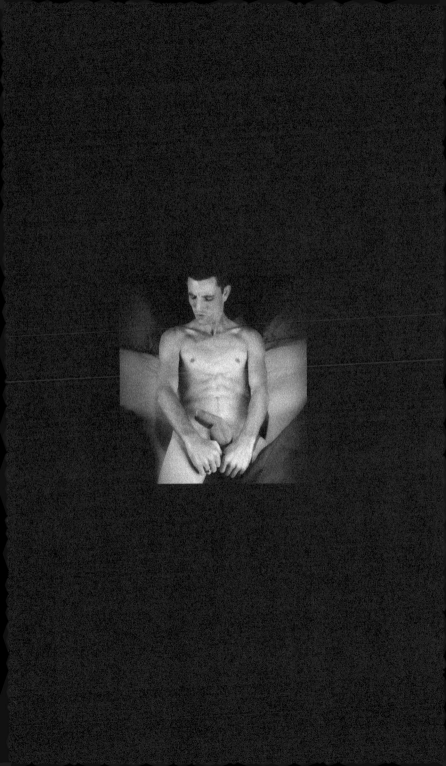

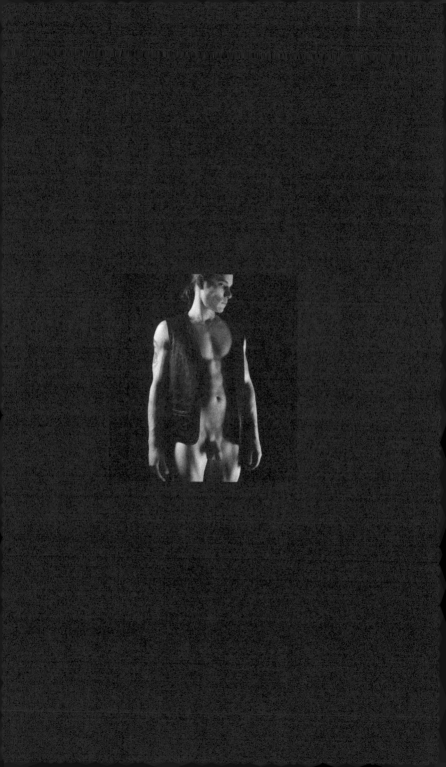

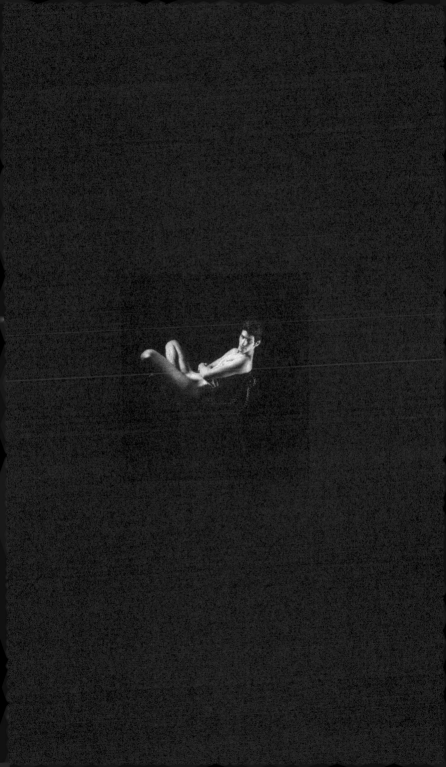

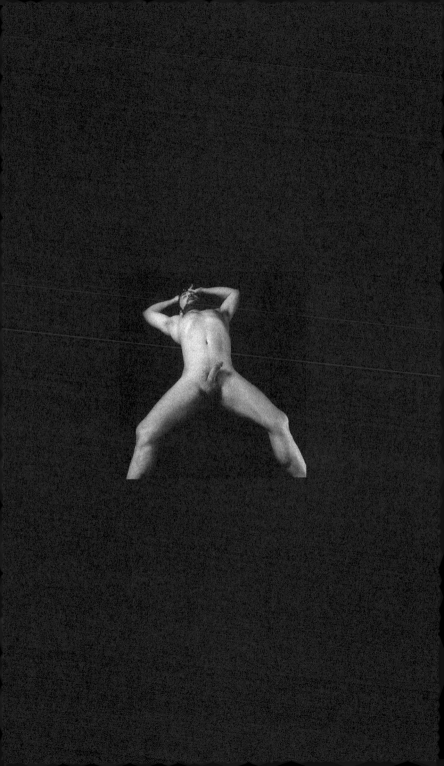

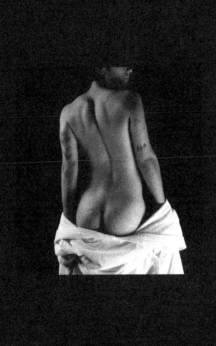

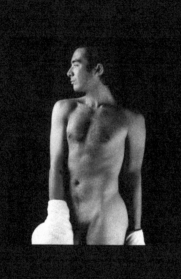

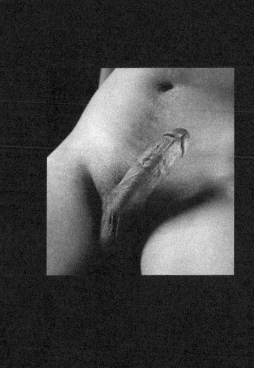

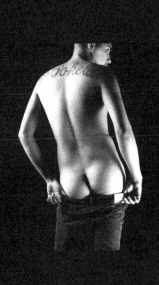

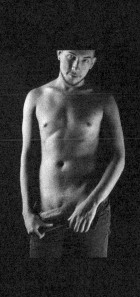

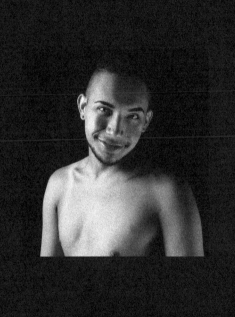

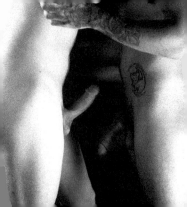

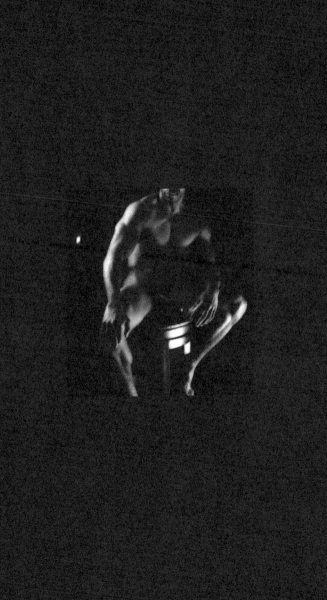

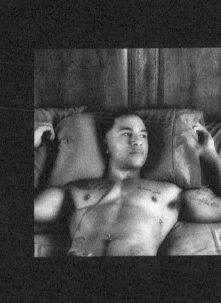